NUAL 2010
K-OFF!

WHAT'S INSIDE...

STATS & FACTS!

RECORD BREAKERS!

Match of the Day reveals football's top record breakers!

MOST WORLD CUPS!
Brazil hold the record for winning five World Cups! They lifted the famous gold trophy in 1958, 1962, 1970, 1994 and 2002!

BECKHAM'S HAT-TRICK!

WORLD CUP TREBLE!
David Beckham is the only England player to score in three different World Cup finals! He netted in the 1998, 2002 and 2006 finals!

YOUNGEST ARSENAL STAR!
Cesc Fabregas became Arsenal's youngest ever player in 2003! The Spain superstar was only 16 years and 177 days old when he played in the Carling Cup against Rotherham!

PAGE 26

QUICKEST FA CUP FINAL GOAL!
Everton striker Louis Saha netted the quickest ever FA Cup final goal in 2009! He scored after just 25 seconds against Chelsea last May!

SUPER SAHA!

MOST TROPHIES!
Man. United's Ryan Giggs is the most successful player in English footy! Giggsy has won 11 Prem titles, two Champo Leagues, four FA Cups and three League Cups!

PREM GOLDEN BOOT!
Thierry Henry is the only striker to top the Prem's scoring charts four times! He won the Golden Boot with Arsenal in 2002, 2004, 2005 and 2006!

MOST EXPENSIVE!
Cristiano Ronaldo became the world's most expensive player in 2009! Real Madrid paid Man. United an amazing £80 million for him!

RECORD REPUBLIC SCORER!
Tottenham star Robbie Keane is the Republic of Ireland's top scorer! He broke the record in 2004 and up to June 2009 he'd scored a wicked 39 goals for his country!

TURN OVER FOR MORE RECORD BREAKERS!

PREMIER LEAGUE HEROES!

MATCH OF THE DAY TEAM OF THE YEAR!

MOTD expert Lee Dixon picks his Prem dream team for 2009!

SOLID AT THE BACK!

ASHLEY COLE
POSITION: Left-back
AGE: 28 CLUB: Chelsea
Ashley started his career at Chelsea with a dip in form, but 2009 was his comeback year! Cole is the best in the business when it comes to buzzing round the opposition and then breaking forward to set up chances!

THE REAL DEAL!

STEAMS FORWARD!

PAGE 18

EDWIN VAN DER SAR
POSITION: Keeper AGE: 39 CLUB: Man. United
United's title win last season was built around their unbeatable defence – and Edwin was a big part of that! He's getting on a bit now, but his reflexes have been as sharp as ever at Old Trafford!

UNITED'S NO.1!

CAPTAIN FANTASTIC!

CRISTIANO RONALDO
POSITION: Winger AGE: 24
CLUB: Real Madrid
The world's number one jetted off to Real Madrid this summer, but it was his big-game skills and storming strikes that took Man. United all the way to the 2009 Premier League title!

GLEN JOHNSON
POSITION: Right-back AGE: 25
CLUB: Liverpool
Johnson's form for Portsmouth at the start of the year earned him a blockbuster summer move to Anfield! He's quick and rarely makes mistakes – and that's why he's also a star for England!

ANFIELD NEW BOY!

RELIABLE RIO!

DEADLY ON THE BALL!

STEVEN GERRARD
POSITION: Midfield
AGE: 29 CLUB: Liverpool
Stevie G loves turning up the heat on the opposition! He plays the game at such pace with first-time passes, bursting runs and long-range piledrivers – he drives the whole Liverpool team to victory!

CESC FABREGAS
POSITION: Midfield AGE: 22
CLUB: Arsenal
The amazing thing about Cesc Fabregas is his composure on the ball and his ability to set up goals for Arsenal. Time and time again in 2009 he showed his class – that's why he's the Gunners' captain!

RIO FERDINAND
POSITION: Centre-back AGE: 30
CLUB: Man. United
There isn't another defender on the planet who can cope with high-pressure situations as well as Rio. He's cool as you like on the ball and his partnership with Vidic in 2009 was formidable!

NEMANJA VIDIC
POSITION: Centre-back AGE: 26
CLUB: Man. United
While Rio's got all the style, Vidic is the man with the brute force in the United back-four! He wins pretty much every ball that he challenges for – and he just had to be in the Match of the Day Team of the Year!

TURN OVER FOR MORE DREAM TEAM STARS!

PLUS LOADS MORE!

TOP 10... TRANSFER

10 LIONEL MESSI
BARCELONA TO INTER MILAN

The rumour: Inter president Massimo Moratti is a massive fan of the little trickster - and he'd smash the world transfer record to sign Messi!

The price: £100m

The chances: 4/10

9 ALEXANDRE PATO
AC MILAN TO CHELSEA

The rumour: Carlo Ancelotti signed the young Brazil star for AC Milan two years ago - and now he's desperate to sign him again! The Chelsea boss reckons Pato is the best young striker in the world!

The price: £35m **The chances:** 8/10

7 JOE COLE
CHELSEA TO TOTTENHAM

The rumour: Chelsea's skills star started his career under Harry Redknapp at West Ham 11 years ago, and now Harry wants him at Tottenham!

The price: £10m **The chances:** 7/10

8 FEDERICO MACHEDA
MAN. UNITED TO LAZIO

The rumour: The teenage striker began his career at Italian club Lazio and if he doesn't get enough chances to play at United, Lazio could make a sneaky bid!

The price: £10m **The chances:** 3/10

6 ALEXANDER HLEB
STUTTGART TO ARSENAL

The rumour: Ex-Arsenal star Hleb is on loan at Stuttgart from Barcelona, but Arsenal could bring him back!

The price: £6m

The chances: 6/10

5 LUKA MODRIC
TOTTENHAM TO MAN. UNITED

The rumour: Man. United have signed Michael Carrick and Dimitar Berbatov from Spurs in recent years - and now Fergie has his eye on their little midfield magician!

The price: £20m

The chances: 7/10

RUMOURS!

THE WORLD'S BIGGEST TRANSFER RUMOUR!

4 FERNANDO TORRES
LIVERPOOL TO REAL MADRID

The rumour: Real Madrid want a Spanish superstar to join their team of Galacticos - and with Raul knocking on a bit they've turned their attention to the Liverpool striker!
The price: £60m
The chances: 3/10

3 JOHN TERRY
CHELSEA TO MAN. CITY

The rumour: City gaffer Mark Hughes failed to land Terry in the summer, but that might not stop him launching a massive bid for the England legend during the January transfer window!
The price: £25m
The chances: 8/10

2 DAVID VILLA
VALENCIA TO LIVERPOOL

1 CESC FABREGAS
ARSENAL TO BARCELONA

The rumour: Barcelona want to bring the silky-skilled playmaker back to the club he played for as a schoolboy! He'd link up with his Spanish team-mates Xavi and Andres Iniesta in an awesome, but tiny, midfield trio at the Nou Camp!
The price: £30m
The chances: 9/10

MAKING THE ULTIMATE STRIKER!

Match of the Day footy boffins have built the ultimate striker - check him out!

EYE FOR GOAL!

DAVID VILLA
He's the best finisher on the planet – simple as that! Villa is lethal from any angle and any distance!

HEADING!

CRISTIANO RONALDO
If the ball gets whipped into the box, then Ron will get on the end of it and bury a power-packed header!

I'll score 100 goals a season!

STRENGTH!

JOHN CAREW
This is one seriously strong dude! Defenders just bounce off the Villa star!

CONTROL!

DIMITAR BERBATOV
Berba is one of the slickest footy stars around! He has a wicked first touch that leaves him in loads of space!

ACCELERATION!

FERNANDO TORRES
The Liverpool man is explosive off the mark! He's already shifting at top speed before the defender realises he's not there!

RIGHT FOOT!

WAYNE ROONEY
His right peg is packed with power but can also pull out some well cheeky chips and tasty tricks when defenders least expect it to happen!

LEFT FOOT!

LIONEL MESSI
Messi's left foot is more magical than Harry Potter! Expect the unexpected from this ace dribbler!

ROONEY
MAN. UNITED

PREMIER LEAGUE SUPERSTAR!
★

WAYNE ROONEY

POSITION Striker
AGE 24
COUNTRY England
VALUE £40 million
TOP SKILLS
Cool finishing and vicious volleys!

MATCH OF THE DAY
MAGAZINE

CRAZY TA

Match of the Day takes a look at the scariest tackles... EVER!

SMACK!

BIFF!

THE HEAD RATTLER!

THWACK!

Look at my new boots!

THE JAW SHAKER!

POW!

Take this, Mr Keeper!

WALLOP!

THE THROAT CHOMPER!

DON'T TRY THESE AT HOME!

THE CHEST CRUNCHER!

MOTTY'S QUIZ!
PREM HEROES!

Hi, I'm BBC footy commentator John Motson! Test your brain power with this brilliant quiz – it's a point for a right answer!

1 How many Prem clubs has Frank Lampard played for?

YOU SAY ....

2 Theo Walcott is a superstar at Arsenal, but where did he start his professional career?

YOU SAY ....

3 How much did Man. City spend to sign Gareth Barry?

YOU SAY ....

4 True or false? Man. United defender Rio Ferdinand joined Leeds in 2000 for £18 million!

YOU SAY ....

5 How many times has Everton's Phil Neville won the Prem?

YOU SAY ....

6 Which country does Tottenham striker Robbie Keane play for?

YOU SAY ....

7 Who's played more games for England – Emile Heskey or Ashley Young?

YOU SAY ....

8 For which London club did Javier Mascherano and Carlos Tevez both make their Prem debuts?

YOU SAY ....

9 How many Champions League finals has Liverpool skipper Steven Gerrard played in?

YOU SAY ....

10 Which Championship club did Stoke sign James Beattie from?

YOU SAY ....

FINAL SCORE...
OUT OF 10

MORE QUIZ FUN ON PAGE 22!

TORRES
LIVERPOOL

PREMIER LEAGUE SUPERSTAR!
★

FERNANDO TORRES

POSITION Striker
AGE 25
COUNTRY Spain
VALUE £45 million
TOP SKILLS
Deadly shooting
and awesome pace!

MATCH OF THE **DAY**
MAGAZINE

THE AMAZING LIFE STORY OF CRISTIANO RONALDO!

Cristiano makes his debut for Sporting Lisbon in 2002 and scores twice! He lights up the Portuguese league in 2002-03!

Rockin' Ron is here!

Man. United snap up the awesome teenager for £12.24 million in 2003!

Nice to meet you, Meeester Fergie!

Did someone tell you it was fancy dress, laddie?

Ronaldo scores the first as United beat Millwall 3-0 in the 2004 FA Cup final! It's his first trophy!

Before this, I'd only ever won a raffle!

Ron tears up the Prem in 2006-07 and he's named the PFA Young Player of the Year and PFA Player of the Year! He's the first player to win both awards in one season since 1977!

What's shinier – my teeth or the trophies?

Man. United win the Prem title in 2007! They finish six points ahead of Chelsea and 21 points ahead of third-placed Liverpool!

More silver for the trophy cabinet!

Ron totally rocks the 2007-08 season! He hits 42 goals in all competitions to win the Golden Boot award as Europe's top goalscorer! It's enough to make him PFA Player of the Year for 2008 as well!

Pow!

GOAL!

I want my mum!

Make it go away!

I'm hiding!

MORE AWESOME MOTD CARTOON FUN ON PAGE 36!

TOP 5...
CELEBRATIONS!

Here are our five favourite Prem celebrations!

5

THE SKY POINT!
Done by... Frank Lampard!
Instructions: Put your arms in the air, now point to the sky and celebrate in style!

THE KNEE SLIDE!
Done by... Steven Gerrard!
Instructions: Run towards the touchline before sliding on your knees with your arms outstretched!

THE FLIP 'N' TWIST!
Done by... Nani!
Instructions: Don't bother trying - you probably won't be able to do this without hurting yourself!

Get in!

4

1

3

Boom! Boom!

THE FLAG PUNCH!
Done by... Tim Cahill!
Instructions: Leg it over to the corner flag and give it a good beating!

THE THUMB SUCK!
Done by... Robinho!
Instructions: All you have to do is stick your thumb in your mouth, suck it and run up the pitch!

2

What's going on at... Man City?

City boss Sheikh Mansour has brought some gifts to the training ground...

Who wants a new pair of boots?

I do! *Me please!* *Yeah!*

Excuse me sir; they don't fit!

Yeah - they're too small!

Have you tried them with the tongues out?

Not your tongues!

Illustration Paul Cemmick

LAMPARD
CHELSEA

PREMIER LEAGUE SUPERSTAR! ★

FRANK LAMPARD

POSITION Midfielder
AGE 31
COUNTRY England
VALUE £14 million
TOP SKILLS
Power-packed shooting
and mega energy!

MATCH OF THE DAY
MAGAZINE

MATCH OF THE DAY
TEAM OF

MOTD expert Lee Dixon picks his Prem dream team for 2009!

SOLID AT THE BACK!

EDWIN VAN DER SAR
POSITION: Keeper **AGE:** 39 **CLUB:** Man. United

United's title win last season was built around their unbeatable defence – and Edwin was a big part of that! He's getting on a bit now, but his reflexes have been as sharp as ever at Old Trafford!

UNITED'S NO.1!

GLEN JOHNSON
POSITION: Right-back **AGE:** 25
CLUB: Liverpool

Johnson's form for Portsmouth at the start of the year earned him a blockbuster summer move to Anfield! He's quick, tough and rarely makes mistakes – and that's why he's also a star for England!

ANFIELD NEW BOY!

RELIABLE RIO!

RIO FERDINAND
POSITION: Centre-back **AGE:** 30
CLUB: Man. United

There isn't another defender on the planet who can cope with high-pressure situations as well as Rio. He's cool as you like on the ball and his partnership with Vidic in 2009 was formidable!

NEMANJA VIDIC
POSITION: Centre-back **AGE:** 28
CLUB: Man. United

While Rio's got all the style, Vidic is the man with the brute force in the United back-four! He wins pretty much every ball that he challenges for – and he just had to be in the Match of the Day Team of the Year!

THE YEAR!

ASHLEY COLE
POSITION: Left-back
AGE: 28 **CLUB:** Chelsea

Ashley started his career at Chelsea with a dip in form, but 2009 was his comeback year! Cole is the best in the business when it comes to buzzing round the opposition and then breaking forward to set up chances!

STEAMS FORWARD!

THE REAL DEAL!

CRISTIANO RONALDO
POSITION: Winger **AGE:** 24
CLUB: Real Madrid

The world's number one jetted off to Real Madrid this summer, but it was his big-game skills and storming strikes that took Man. United all the way to the 2009 Premier League title!

CAPTAIN FANTASTIC!

STEVEN GERRARD
POSITION: Midfield
AGE: 29
CLUB: Liverpool

Stevie G loves turning up the heat on the opposition! He plays the game at such pace with first-time passes, bursting runs and long-range piledrivers – he drives the whole Liverpool team to victory!

DEADLY ON THE BALL!

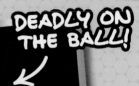

CESC FABREGAS
POSITION: Midfield **AGE:** 22
CLUB: Arsenal

The amazing thing about Cesc Fabregas is his composure on the ball and his ability to set up goals for Arsenal. Time and time again in 2009 he showed his class – that's why he's the Gunners' captain!

TURN OVER FOR MORE DREAM TEAM STARS!

WICKED WINGER!

GOAL CRAZY!

FERNANDO TORRES
POSITION: Striker **AGE:** 25
CLUB: Liverpool

Liverpool's title challenge stumbled while Torres was out injured last season – when he returned, it sparked back into life. Torres scores all sorts of goals – and in just two years he's become a Liverpool legend!

ASHLEY YOUNG
POSITION: Winger **AGE:** 24
CLUB: Aston Villa

Villa manager Martin O'Neill says the winger is a genius – and we can see why! His crosses whip into the box at amazing speed and his searing runs leave desperate defenders trailing in his wake!

DIXON'S TEAM!

NATURAL FINISHER!

NICOLAS ANELKA
POSITION: Striker
AGE: 30
CLUB: Chelsea

What Anelka lacks in skill he more than makes up for with his natural eye for goal! His positional sense in the box is class and he always puts his chances away – that's why he finished the season as the Prem's top scorer with 19 goals!

VAN DER SAR

JOHNSON

COLE

FERDINAND

VIDIC

RONALDO

FABREGAS

YOUNG

GERRARD

TORRES

ANELKA

ARSHAVIN
ARSENAL

PREMIER
LEAGUE
SUPERSTAR!
★

GOAL KINGS!

How much do you know about the world's top strikers? Score a point for each answer you get right!

1 Which country does Arsenal's Robin van Persie play for?

YOU SAY ....

2 Chelsea signed Didier Drogba from which French club?

YOU SAY ....

3 True or false? Man. United striker Michael Owen is England's all-time top goalscorer?

YOU SAY ....

4 Which Liverpool striker scored the winner for Spain in the final of Euro 2008 against Germany?

YOU SAY ....

5 Thierry Henry used to play in the Prem, but for which club?

YOU SAY ....

6 How much did Man. United pay Tottenham for Bulgarian striker Dimitar Berbatov?

YOU SAY ....

7 Which Italian team does Brazil striker Pato play for?

YOU SAY ....

8 Who scored Everton's only goal in the 2009 FA Cup Final?

YOU SAY ....

9 For which club did Jermain Defoe make his Premier League debut?

YOU SAY ....

10 How many Champo League finals has Samuel Eto'o scored in?

YOU SAY ....

FINAL SCORE... OUT OF 10

ANSWERS

SEE HOW MANY YOU GOT RIGHT! 1 Holland, 2 Marseille, 3 False, 4 Fernando Torres, 5 Arsenal, 6 £30.75 million, 7 AC Milan, 8 Louis Saha, 9 West Ham, 10 Two.

MORE QUIZ FUN ON PAGE 30!

22

KEANE
TOTTENHAM

PREMIER LEAGUE SUPERSTAR! ★

ROBBIE KEANE

POSITION Striker
AGE 29
COUNTRY Republic of Ireland
VALUE £15 million
TOP SKILLS Sharp movement and lethal shooting!

MATCH OF THE DAY MAGAZINE

Skills! PLAY LI SUPER STR

Match of the Day reveals the top secret tips to being a goal machine like these Prem strikers!

1 Rooney moves around to give defenders big problems! Drop into midfield, or go to the wing, to get the ball…

…pass to a team-mate and then race into the box for the return pass! Now you're in the goalscoring danger zone!

2 Torres is the best in the world at scoring when he's one-on-one with a keeper…

… run fast at goal – it makes it harder for the keeper to grab the ball – and be confident in yourself. Side-foot a shot early or take the ball round the keeper and coolly finish!

KE A...
IKER!

3 Drogba uses his power to hold up the ball for his team-mates...

...keep your body in between the defender and the ball and look up to see which team-mate you can lay the ball off to!

4 The secret to a mega header is timing! Jump at the right time to meet the ball, and try to get higher than your opponent...

...be brave and keep your eyes on the ball until you head it with your forehead!

Turn to page 34 for more ace skills tips!

5 TOP STRIKERS!

DAVID VILLA
Valencia
Top skill: Deadly finishing!

SAMUEL ETO'O
Inter Milan
Top skill: Long-range blasts!

KARIM BENZEMA
Real Madrid
Top skill: Turbo shooting!

ZLATAN IBRAHIMOVIC
Barcelona
Top skill: Mint footwork!

DIMITAR BERBATO
Man. United
Top skill: Ace ball control!

RECORD BREAKERS

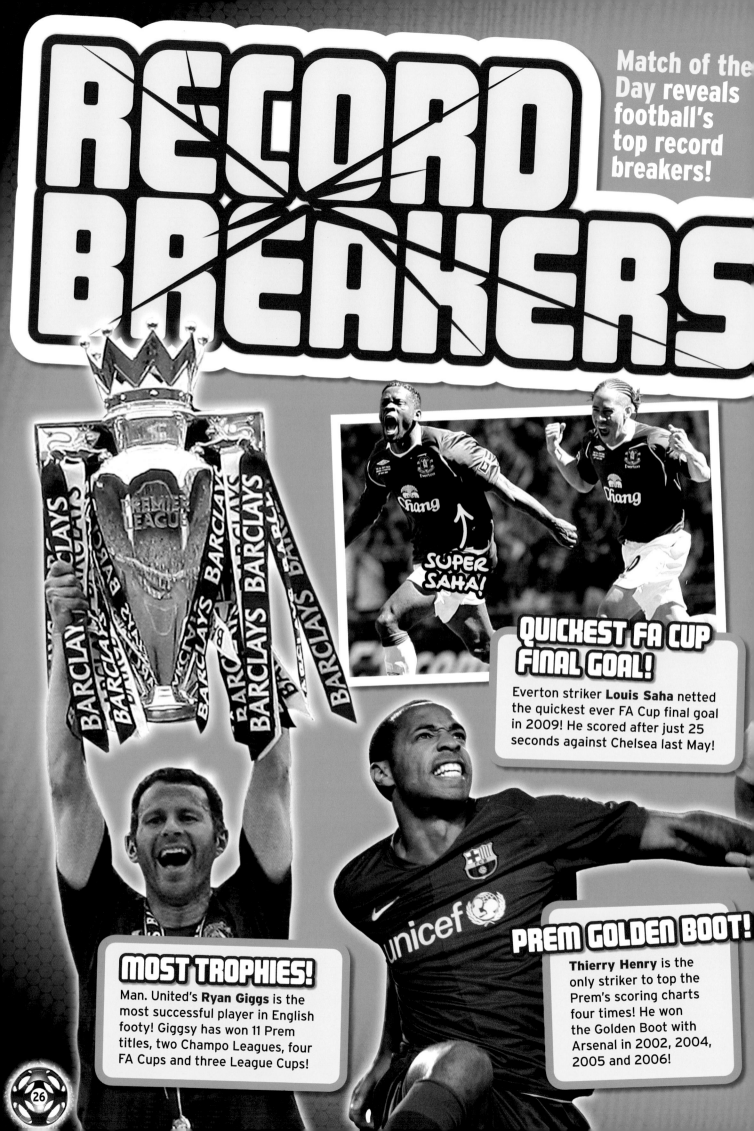

QUICKEST FA CUP FINAL GOAL!

Everton striker **Louis Saha** netted the quickest ever FA Cup final goal in 2009! He scored after just 25 seconds against Chelsea last May!

MOST TROPHIES!

Man. United's **Ryan Giggs** is the most successful player in English footy! Giggsy has won 11 Prem titles, two Champo Leagues, four FA Cups and three League Cups!

PREM GOLDEN BOOT!

Thierry Henry is the only striker to top the Prem's scoring charts four times! He won the Golden Boot with Arsenal in 2002, 2004, 2005 and 2006!

SUPER SAHA!

MOST WORLD CUPS!

Brazil hold the record for winning five World Cups! They lifted the famous gold trophy in 1958, 1962, 1970, 1994 and 2002!

BECKHAM'S HAT-TRICK!

WORLD CUP TREBLE!

David Beckham is the only England player to score in three different World Cup finals! He netted in the 1998, 2002 and 2006 finals!

YOUNGEST ARSENAL STAR!

Cesc Fabregas became Arsenal's youngest ever player in 2003! The Spain superstar was only 16 years and 177 days old when he played in the Carling Cup against Rotherham!

CESC IS FAB!

MOST EXPENSIVE!

Cristiano Ronaldo became the world's most expensive player in 2009! Real Madrid paid Man. United an amazing £80 million for him!

RECORD REPUBLIC SCORER!

Tottenham star **Robbie Keane** is the Republic of Ireland's top scorer! He broke the record in 2004 and up to June 2009 he'd scored a wicked 39 goals for his country!

TURN OVER FOR MORE RECORD BREAKERS!

RECORD BREAKERS!

GOAL KING!

RECORD WORLD CUP SCORER!

Brazil ace **Ronaldo** has bagged 15 goals at World Cup finals! The Corinthians star set the record at the 2006 World Cup!

MOST LEAGUE CUP WINS!

Liverpool have won the League Cup seven times in their history! The Reds last won it in 2003 when Steven Gerrard scored in the final!

ITALY LEGEND!

MOST ITALIAN CLUB GAMES!

AC Milan legend **Paolo Maldini** retired in 2009 after playing his 902nd game for them - no player has played more games for one Italian club than him!

THE KING RULES!

QUICKEST PREM GOAL!

Tottenham's **Ledley King** scored the quickest Prem League goal - just ten seconds after kick-off against Bradford back in 2000!

MOST SCOTTISH TITLES!

Rangers have won Scotland's top division a record 52 times! The Glasgow giants picked up another SPL title in May!

BIGGEST SCORING GAME!

When **Portsmouth** beat Reading 7-4 in 2007, it easily became the highest-scoring game in Premier League history with 11 goals!

MOST EURO CUP WINS!

Real Madrid have won the Champions League a record nine times! They first won the cup, which used to be called the European Cup, way back in 1956!

YOUNG LION!

RECORD CLEAN SHEETS!

Keeper **Edwin van der Sar** set a new British record last season when he went 1,311 minutes without letting in a goal for Man. United!

YOUNGEST ENGLAND PLAYER!

Theo Walcott is England's youngest player! He first played for the Three Lions when he was just 17 years and 75 days old back in 2006!

MOTTY'S QUIZ!
SUPERSTARS WORDSEARCH!

Find these 25 megastars - it's four points for each one!

```
B L K L H W C P X C A H M F F D H
E M D R R Z D F A B R E G A S P O
R R E K Q O R X T P J Z Z F W O U
B I I S C H O H E L A M P A R D I
A B B D S R G N V H E N R Y H Q N
T E E T D I B N E M Y Z P Y X C I
O R N O K H A K Z Y E K H Z I Y E
V Y Z R O N A L D I N H O V K I S
O W E R Z M Y J A V Y G O A T B T
R W M E A G U E R O H M K T R E A
X H A S K E M C S G I A O G O C E
G E R R A R D E H H K T A T N K E
S R O B I N H O A O Z P A C A H B
E O S K O C K R V Q W P H C L A H
N Q I U D T B R I V I L L A D M D
W I A L K I A L N X Q Z L K O G C
K O H M F E R D I N A N D C O P N
```

Benzema!

Ibrahimovic!

Kaka!

Ronaldinho!

Henry!

Totti!

- AGUERO
- ARSHAVIN
- BECKHAM
- BENZEMA
- BERBATOV
- DROGBA
- FABREGAS
- FERDINAND
- GERRARD
- HENRY
- IBRAHIMOVIC
- INIESTA
- KAKA
- LAMPARD
- MESSI
- PATO
- RIBERY
- ROBINHO
- RONALDINHO
- RONALDO
- ROONEY
- TEVEZ
- TORRES
- TOTTI
- VILLA

ANSWERS

FINAL SCORE...
OUT OF 100

CAHILL
EVERTON

TIM CAHILL

POSITION Midfielder
AGE 29
COUNTRY Australia
VALUE £7 million
TOP SKILLS
Power heading and slick passing!

MATCH OF THE **DAY**
MAGAZINE

STARS AND THEIR CARS!

Match of the Day reveals what flash cars the footy stars drive!

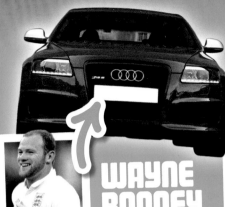

WAYNE ROONEY
MAN. UNITED & ENGLAND

CAR Audi RS6
PRICE £80,000
TOP SPEED 155mph
0-60MPH 4.6 seconds
FLASH RATING 7/10

KAKA
REAL MADRID & BRAZIL

CAR Audi R8
PRICE £78,000
TOP SPEED 187mph
0-60MPH 4.6 seconds
FLASH RATING 8/10

ROBBIE KEANE
TOTTENHAM & REP. OF IRELAND

CAR Range Rover
PRICE £70,000
TOP SPEED 130mph
0-60MPH 7.1 seconds
FLASH RATING 5/10

ROBINHO
MAN. CITY & BRAZIL

CAR Lamborghini Gallardo
PRICE £131,000
TOP SPEED 195mph
0-60MPH 4.3 seconds
FLASH RATING 9/10

CRISTIANO RONALDO
REAL MADRID & PORTUGAL

CAR Bentley Continental
PRICE £130,500
TOP SPEED 195mph
0-60MPH 4.8 seconds
FLASH RATING 8/10

EL-HADJI DIOUF
BLACKBURN & SENEGAL

CAR SLR McLaren
PRICE £420,000
TOP SPEED 207mph
0-60MPH 3.6 seconds
FLASH RATING 10/10

Skills! PLAY LI
QUALITY W

If you want to learn how to rip it up out wide, follow Match of the Day's wicked step-by-step guide!

1 Ronaldo's favourite trick is 'the chop' – he uses it to cut back across defenders into space as soon as he gets possession of the ball…

2 You can be a top wide man with pace and acceleration – Theo Walcott uses his speed to get past tackles…

…if a defender is tight to you when you get the ball, knock it into the space behind him and go head-to-head in a sprint! If you're fast, you'll beat him!

…as the ball comes into you, use the inside of your foot to stab it quickly back the other way behind your standing leg. This will leave the defender off balance and you a path to goal!

KE A ... NGER!

5 TOP WINGERS!

LIONEL MESSI
Barcelona
Top skill: Unbelievable dribbling!

3 Crossing the ball well is one of the most important skills for a winger to have...

...when Ashley Young hits a lethal cross into the box, he makes sure he beats the first man by whipping the ball across at pace, bending it towards the far post. Copy him and you won't go far wrong!

ANTONIO VALENCIA
Man. United
Top skill: Rocket shots on goal!

FRANCK RIBERY
Bayern Munich
Top skill: Lightning pace on the ball!

4 If you want to be a big part of your attack, you need to be a reliable goalscorer and get into the box...

...if you can't make a pass or get a cross in, then try to beat the defender and race into the box. Use different tricks to get past the opposition and shooting early can catch the keeper out!

AARON LENNON
Tottenham
Top skill: Non-stop running all game!

Turn to page 40 for more footy tips!

ROBINHO
Man. City
Top skill: Bamboozling stepovers!

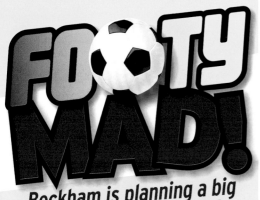

FOOTY MAD!

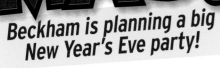

Beckham is planning a big New Year's Eve party!

Becks calls his pal Cristiano Ronaldo...

Hey Ron, I'm staying at my pad in Madrid – wanna come over for a New Year's pool party?

You bet, Dave!

Who else is gonna be there?

...there'll be loads of top stars there so be ready for the challenge!

Bonjour, Ronny!

Ronaldo heads to his local pool to get some practice in...

Hey Drogba, I always knew you were a *diver!*

On his way home...

SWIMWEAR SALE !

A-ha, I'd better pick up some new trunks if I want to impress Becks!

It's the Wolves boss...

What are you doing here, Mick?

I'm looking for something to help Wolves stay *afloat* in the Prem!

LIFEJAC

Next week at Beckham's house...

Hi Becks – where can I get changed?

EL BECKO PALACE

First door on the left, then get upstairs and join the party!

I thought you said it was a pool party!

It is, I just bought a new *pool table!*

What a goon!

He's definitely not gonna *sink* any pots with that rubber ring!

Illustration Steve McGarry

ADEBAYOR
MAN. CITY

PREMIER LEAGUE SUPERSTAR! ★

EMMANUEL ADEBAYOR

POSITION Striker
AGE 25
COUNTRY Togo
VALUE £25 million
TOP SKILLS
Acrobatic volleys and crisp control!

MATCH OF THE DAY
MAGAZINE

"MY FAVE T

The Prem's top stars tell Match of the Day what they love to watch on television!

JAMES BEATTIE
STOKE

JAMES SAYS: "I've got to say, I do like Britain's Got Talent! That's probably my favourite TV show. If I had to go on it, I'd just pull stupid faces or make funny noises!"

Can you sing and dance, Beatts?

TIM HOWARD
EVERTON

TIM SAYS: "My favourite TV show has to be Grey's Anatomy! It's an American medical drama – a bit like ER – I think it's on one of the Sky channels. I really love watching it!"

GREY'S ANATOMY

HOWARD'S A FAN!

JONNY EVANS
MAN. UNITED

JONNY SAYS: "I like The Inbetweeners! It's a really funny comedy! I watch it every week – I'm really into it. Shameless is also a bit of a favourite of mine!"

Jonny looks like he's still at school!

V SHOW!!

Find out what we like to watch!

CHRIS KIRKLAND
WIGAN

CHRIS SAYS: "It's got to be 24, although I also like EastEnders! I bought the DVD box sets of 24 to take with me on the pre-season tours, because you're away for a while and that really helped pass the time!"

The clock is ticking, Chris!

ROQUE SANTA CRUZ
MAN. CITY

ROQUE SAYS: "X Factor is pretty much the only TV programme I watch! Everyone talks about it when it's on, so you can't avoid it. It can be funny when some people come on and can't sing! It's nice to see that so many people are into music though!"

GLEN JOHNSON
LIVERPOOL

GLEN SAYS: "I'm a big fan of Only Fools and Horses, even though I don't really watch that much TV these days! That programme still absolutely cracks me up! I've got the whole lot on DVD box set!"

Lavverly jabbly! Glen likes us!

If you want to learn how to be a solid defender, follow Match of the Day's awesome step-by-step skills guide!

1 Never take risks at the back! The most important job for any defender is to stop the opposition from scoring goals – so hanging around on the ball in your own penalty area is a big no-no…

2 Slide tackles look good – but if you don't win the ball, you'll look like a right mug! It'll also give the attacker a free run…

…stay on your feet to intercept the ball. But if the striker gets it, don't give him any space – keep your eyes on the ball and time your tackle!

4 All defenders need to be ace at heading! Lots of balls will be fired forward or whipped into the box at head height – and you've got to be able to head it clear…

…as soon as you get the ball, look up to see if you can pass it to a team-mate! If there's no-one in space and you're being closed down, smash the ball as far up the pitch as possible!

KE A... FENDER!

3 The best full-backs in the world are as good going forward as they are at defending! You obviously need to be a top tackler and good defensively – but you'll also be expected to get up the wing to help attacks...

...when your winger has the ball, overlap him. The opposition full-back will be marking your team-mate and this will give you a free run up the wing! Try to make sure your crosses are top notch!

...spring up and use your body strength to power through players! Attack the ball with the middle of your forehead – and remember the key is distance and height!

Turn to page 52 for more footy tips!

5 TOP DEFENDERS

RIO FERDINAND
Man. United
Top skill: Great ball control!

CURTIS DAVIES
Aston Villa
Top skill: Ace acceleration!

SERGIO RAMOS
Real Madrid
Top skill: Tough tackling!

KOLO TOURE
Man. City
Top skill: Well-timed tackles!

MAICON
Inter Milan
Top skill: Ace crossing!

DID YOU K

Match of the Day reveals ten fascinating footy facts!

All right, Unc!

ALMOST A GUNNER!

Tottenham manager Harry Redknapp is the uncle of Chelsea and England midfielder Frank Lampard!

Alex Ferguson nearly became Arsenal manager in 1986 - but he decided to take the Man. United job instead!

GOAL KING!

The biggest World Cup crowd ever was in 1950 for the match between Brazil and Uruguay! The game drew a mega crowd of 174,000!

Blackburn keeper Paul Robinson has scored two goals in his career!

MOTTY'S QUIZ!

SPOT THE STARS!

10 Prem hardmen are hiding here! It's a point for each one you find!

TICK THE PLAYERS YOU'VE FOUND!

- JOHN CAREW
- LEE CATTERMOLE
- KEVIN DAVIES
- SYLVAIN DISTIN
- ABDOULAYE FAYE
- MAROUANE FELLAINI
- STEVEN GERRARD
- LEDLEY KING
- WAYNE ROONEY
- CHRISTOPHER SAMBA

FINAL SCORE... OUT OF 10

44

MORE QUIZ FUN ON PAGE 54!

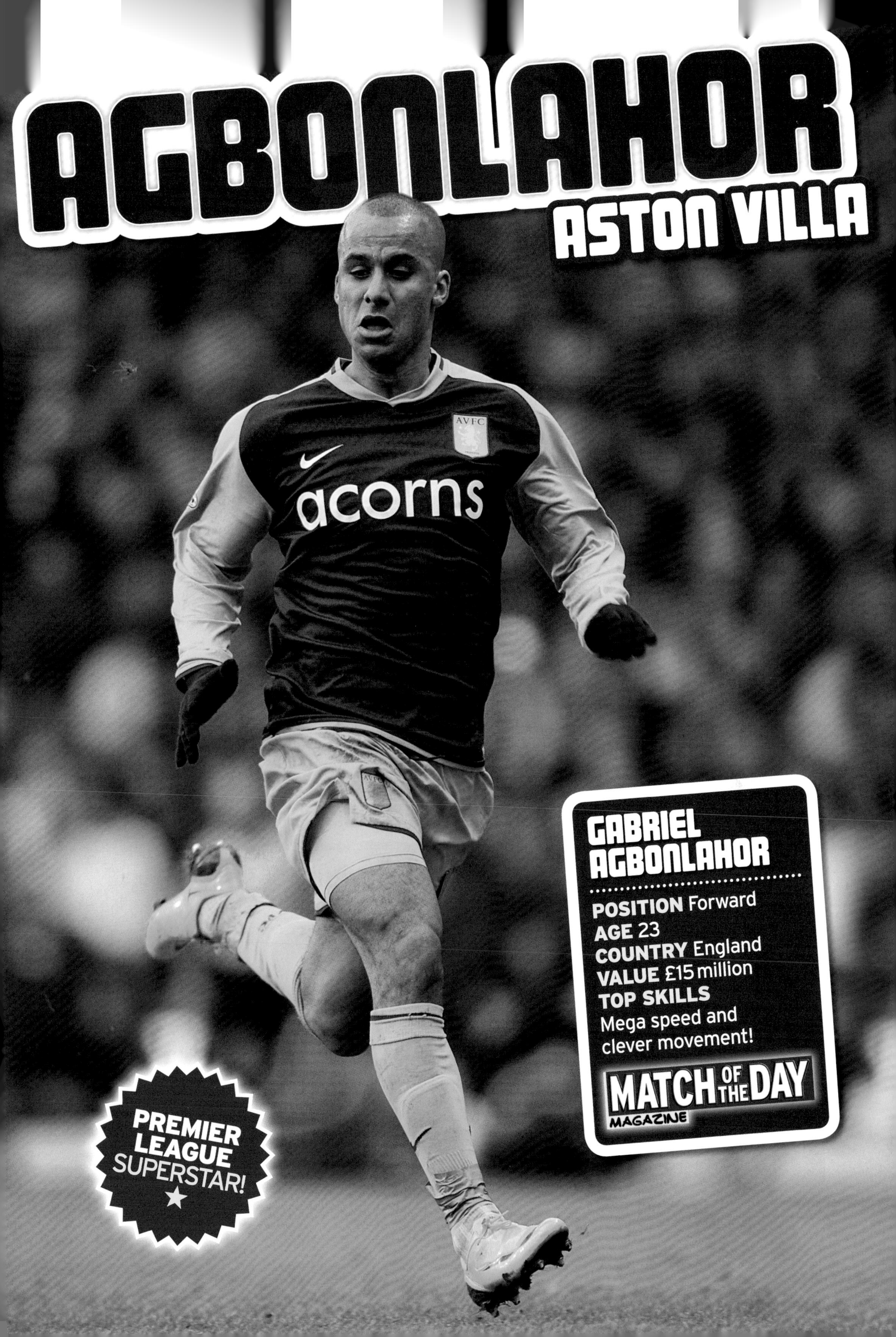

AGBONLAHOR
ASTON VILLA
acorns
GABRIEL AGBONLAHOR
POSITION Forward
AGE 23
COUNTRY England
VALUE £15 million
TOP SKILLS
Mega speed and clever movement!
MATCH OF THE DAY MAGAZINE
PREMIER LEAGUE SUPERSTAR!

Take a look at these super strikes from last season

ANFIELD STUNNER!

1

FERNANDO TORRES

CLUB **Liverpool** DATE **11 April 2009**
Liverpool's Spanish superstar turned on the style against Blackburn when he controlled a long ball on his chest and then volleyed it over the keeper!

GIGGS FIRES HOME!

3

CARLTON COLE

CLUB **West Ham**
DATE **4 March 2009**
West Ham pinged the ball around the Wigan defence, then Cole finished off the move with a cool strike into the bottom corner!

RYAN GIGGS

CLUB **Man. United**
DATE **8 February 2009**
Giggsy cut in from the left wing and curled a shot through a crowd of West Ham players to win the game!

CARLTON'S FINISH

THE SEASON!

picked out by Gary Lineker and the MOTD gang!

NET BUSTER!

VAN'S THE MAN!

4 PAUL KONCHESKY

CLUB **Fulham**
DATE **18 January 2009**
Konchesky silenced West Ham with this 30-yard rocket! He picked up the ball in his own half, bombed on and cracked it into the top corner!

5 ROBIN VAN PERSIE

CLUB **Arsenal**
DATE **21 December 2008**
Van Persie controlled a long ball, then turned and smashed it past Liverpool keeper Pepe Reina!

JOHNSON'S ROCKET!

MOTD'S GOAL OF THE SEASON! ★

GLEN JOHNSON 6

CLUB **Portsmouth**
DATE **22 November 2008**
When the ball fell into Glen's path after Hull cleared, he chested it and volleyed it into the top corner from 25 yards out – while still running!

TURN OVER FOR MORE GOALS OF THE SEASON!

GOALS OF THE SEASON!

BENTLEY BLASTS IT!

JENAS 8

7

DAVID BENTLEY

CLUB **Spurs** DATE **29 October 2008**
Bentley let loose a 40-yard monster strike against his ex-club Arsenal! He saw Gunners keeper Almunia off his line, flicked the ball up and volleyed it over his head and into the goal!

RICARDO FULLER

8

CLUB **Stoke** DATE **23 August 2008**
Fuller stunned Aston Villa when he flicked Liam Lawrence's pass over Martin Laursen's head and then drilled it in from a tight angle!

LONG-RANGE BEAUTY!

SUPER SKILLS!

KAROO

9

GEOVANNI

CLUB **Hull** DATE **27 September 2008**
Arsenal thought there was no danger when Geo had the ball 25 yards out! Seconds later the ball was in the top corner after an awesome strike!

GOALS OF THE SEASON!
MY FAVE 3 GOALS!

1st ....

2nd ....

3rd ....

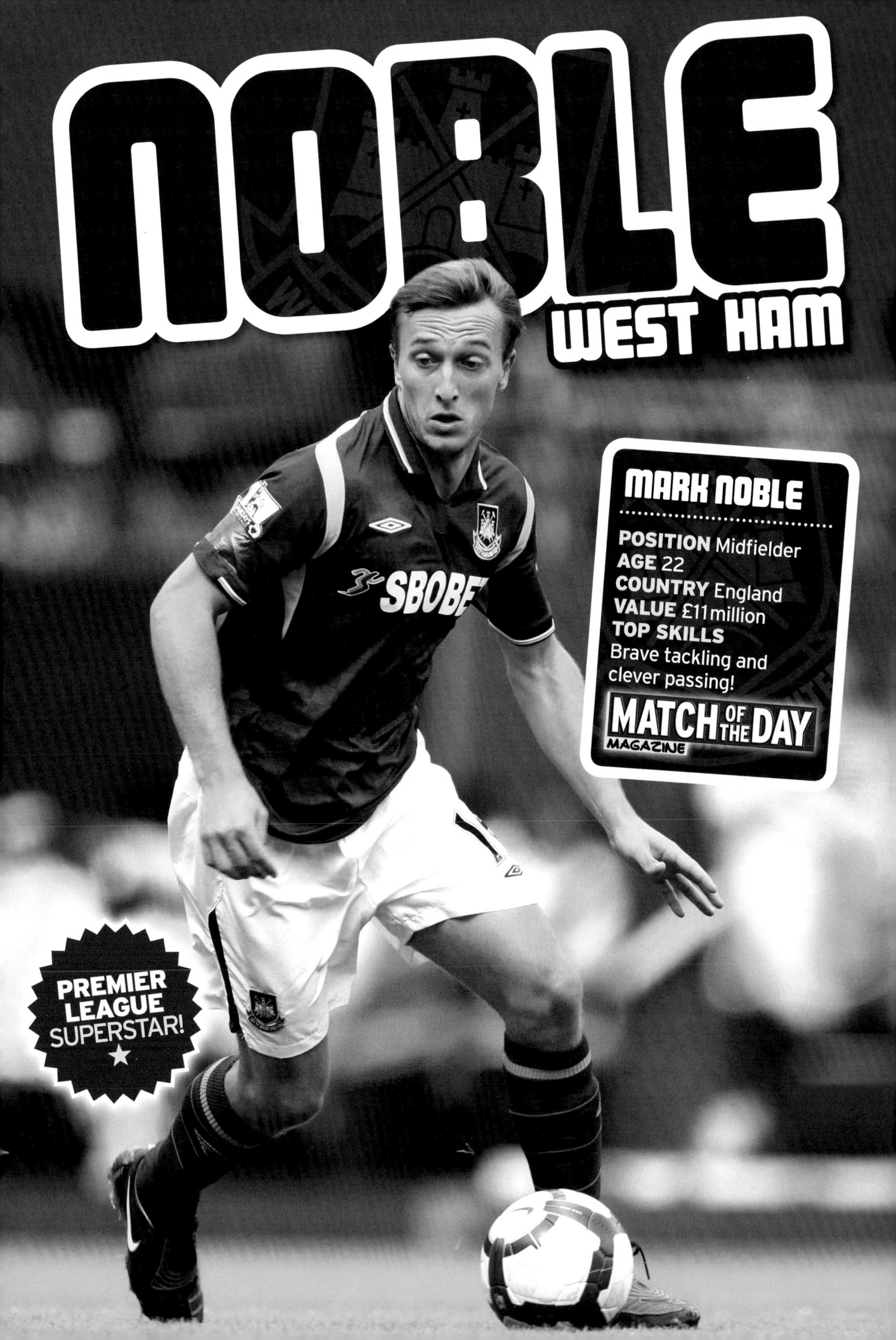

NOBLE
WEST HAM

MARK NOBLE

POSITION Midfielder
AGE 22
COUNTRY England
VALUE £11 million
TOP SKILLS
Brave tackling and
clever passing!

MATCH OF THE DAY
MAGAZINE

PREMIER
LEAGUE
SUPERSTAR!
★

IF FOOTY STARS WERE... POP STARS!

Match of the Day wonders what footy stars and pop stars have in common!

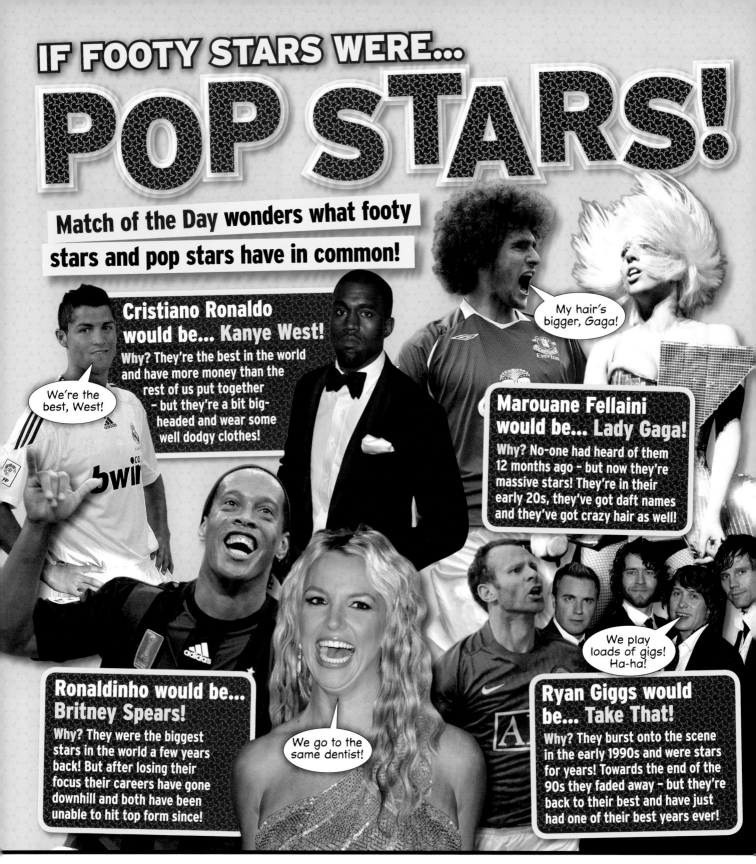

Cristiano Ronaldo would be... Kanye West!

Why? They're the best in the world and have more money than the rest of us put together – but they're a bit big-headed and wear some well dodgy clothes!

Marouane Fellaini would be... Lady Gaga!

Why? No-one had heard of them 12 months ago – but now they're massive stars! They're in their early 20s, they've got daft names and they've got crazy hair as well!

Ronaldinho would be... Britney Spears!

Why? They were the biggest stars in the world a few years back! But after losing their focus their careers have gone downhill and both have been unable to hit top form since!

Ryan Giggs would be... Take That!

Why? They burst onto the scene in the early 1990s and were stars for years! Towards the end of the 90s they faded away – but they're back to their best and have just had one of their best years ever!

What's going on at... Real Madrid?

MURPHY
FULHAM

PREMIER LEAGUE SUPERSTAR! ★

DANNY MURPHY

POSITION Midfielder
AGE 32
COUNTRY England
VALUE £2 million
TOP SKILLS
Ace passing and
slick free-kicks!

MATCH OF THE DAY
MAGAZINE

Skills! PLAY LI MEGA MIDI

Do you want to become an all-round superstar midfielder? Then check out Match of the Day's top tips!

1 You've got to have loads of variety in your passing…

…mark out a target and aim passes towards it from distance to perfect your long passing. Practise your pass-and-move game, play some one-touch footy with your mate – every time you pass, move into space for the return ball!

2 It gets tough on the pitch, so you've got to prove you have the strength to get stuck in with the big boys…

…being tough in the tackle isn't about being the biggest guy on the pitch – you need to watch the ball and time your tackles well if you want to win the ball and make a pass!

KE A... FIELDER!

3

Michael Essien's nickname is The Train because he's got so much energy...

...you need a high level of stamina to perform like Essien and that means lots of running. When you jog in training, make sure you do some short bursts of sprinting every couple of minutes to get your body used to a proper game of footy!

4

If you play as an attacking midfielder, you need to learn how to pick the right moment to break forward into the box for a shooting chance...

...Everton's Tim Cahill is an expert at this. Sometimes when his team attacks, he stays outside the box and waits for a cross to come in. If the ball drops loose, he bursts into action – copy him and you'll be a total menace going forward!

Turn to page 70 for more skills tips!

5 TOP MIDFIELDERS

KAKA
Real Madrid
Top skill: Classic close control!

ANDRES INIESTA
Barcelona
Top skill: Pinpoint through balls!

FRANK LAMPARD
Chelsea
Top skill: Long-range piledrivers!

MICHAEL CARRICK
Man. United
Top skill: Bossing the midfield!

XAVI
Barcelona
Top skill: Perfect passing!

MOTTY'S QUIZ!
BRAZIL STARS!

What do you know about these brilliant Brazil stars? Give yourself a point for each answer you get right!

1 How old is Man. City's Brazilian star Robinho?

YOU SAY ....

2 From which club did Real Madrid sign Kaka this summer?

YOU SAY ....

3 When was the last time Brazil won the World Cup final – 2006, 2002 or 1998?

YOU SAY ....

4 Which European club does Brazil keeper Julio Cesar play for?

YOU SAY ....

5 Can you name Man. United's Brazilian midfield superkid?

YOU SAY ....

6 What is the name of Brazil's legendary big stadium in Rio?

YOU SAY ....

7 How much did Barca pay Sevilla for Dani Alves - £25 million, £30 million or £35 million?

YOU SAY ....

8 In which position does Heurelho Gomes play for Tottenham?

YOU SAY ....

9 True or false? Brazilian legend Ronaldo played for both Real Madrid and Barcelona!

YOU SAY ....

10 How many times has Ronaldinho won the Champions League?

YOU SAY ....

FINAL SCORE...
OUT OF 10

54

MORE QUIZ FUN ON PAGE 66!

ROBERTS
BLACKBURN

PREMIER LEAGUE SUPERSTAR! ★

JASON ROBERTS

POSITION Striker
AGE 31
COUNTRY Grenada
VALUE £2 million
TOP SKILLS
Awesome power and
great acceleration!

MATCH OF THE **DAY**
MAGAZINE

CROWN
PAINTS

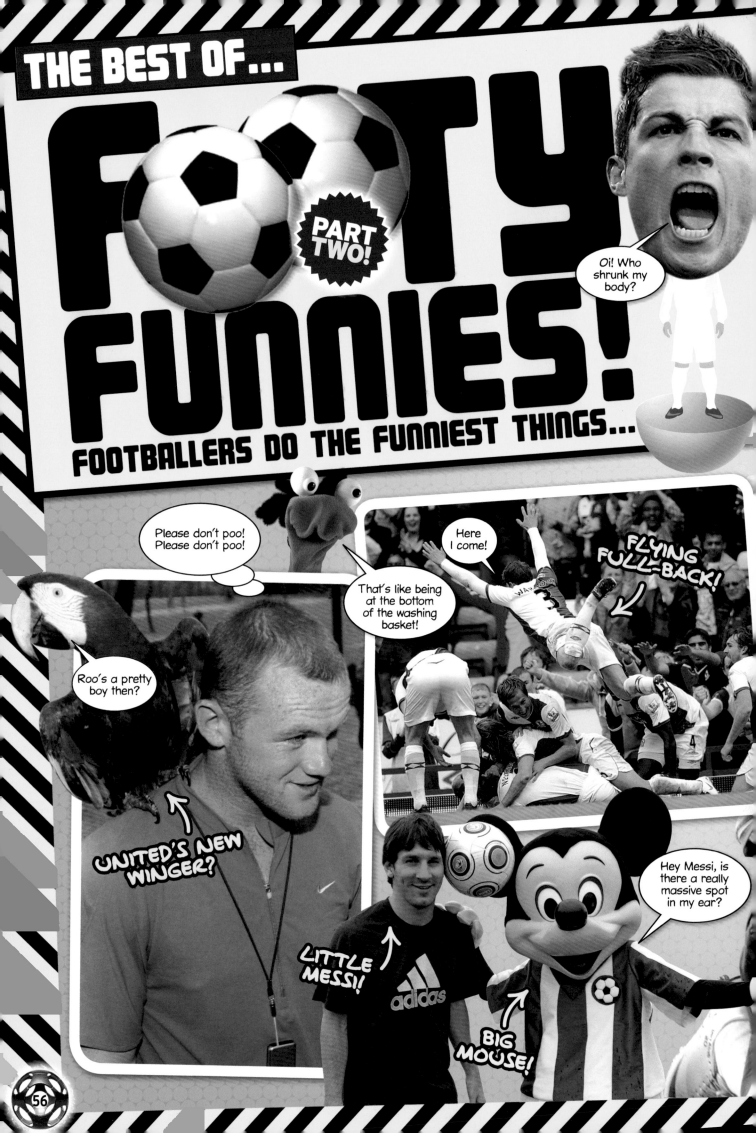

MATCH OF THE DAY STARS AS PLAYERS!

You see them every Saturday on the TV – but what were the MOTD experts like as players?

COOL DEFENDER!

MARK LAWRENSON

He was a... centre-back!

He played for... Tampa Bay Rowdies, Barnet, Liverpool, Brighton, Preston

Republic of Ireland games/goals: 39/5

He played like... Jamie Carragher!

Today he'd be worth... £17 million

Did you know? Lawro won the League five times with Liverpool in the 1980s!

FLYING FULL-BACK!

LEE DIXON

He was a... right-back!

He played for... Arsenal, Stoke, Bury, Chester, Burnley

England games/goals: 22/1

He played like... Gary Neville!

Today he'd be worth... £10 million

Did you know? Lee won four league titles with Arsenal!

ALAN HANSEN

He was a... centre-back!

He played for... Liverpool, Partick Thistle

Scotland games/goals: 26/0

He played like... Rio Ferdinand!

Today he'd be worth... £20 million

Did you know? Alan won the European Cup three times!

TOP TACKLER!

LETHAL STRIKER!

GARY LINEKER

He was a... striker!

He played for... Grampus Eight, Tottenham, Barcelona, Everton, Leicester

England games/goals: 80/48

He played like... Michael Owen!

Today he'd be worth... £32 million

Did you know? Gary finished top scorer at the 1986 World Cup!

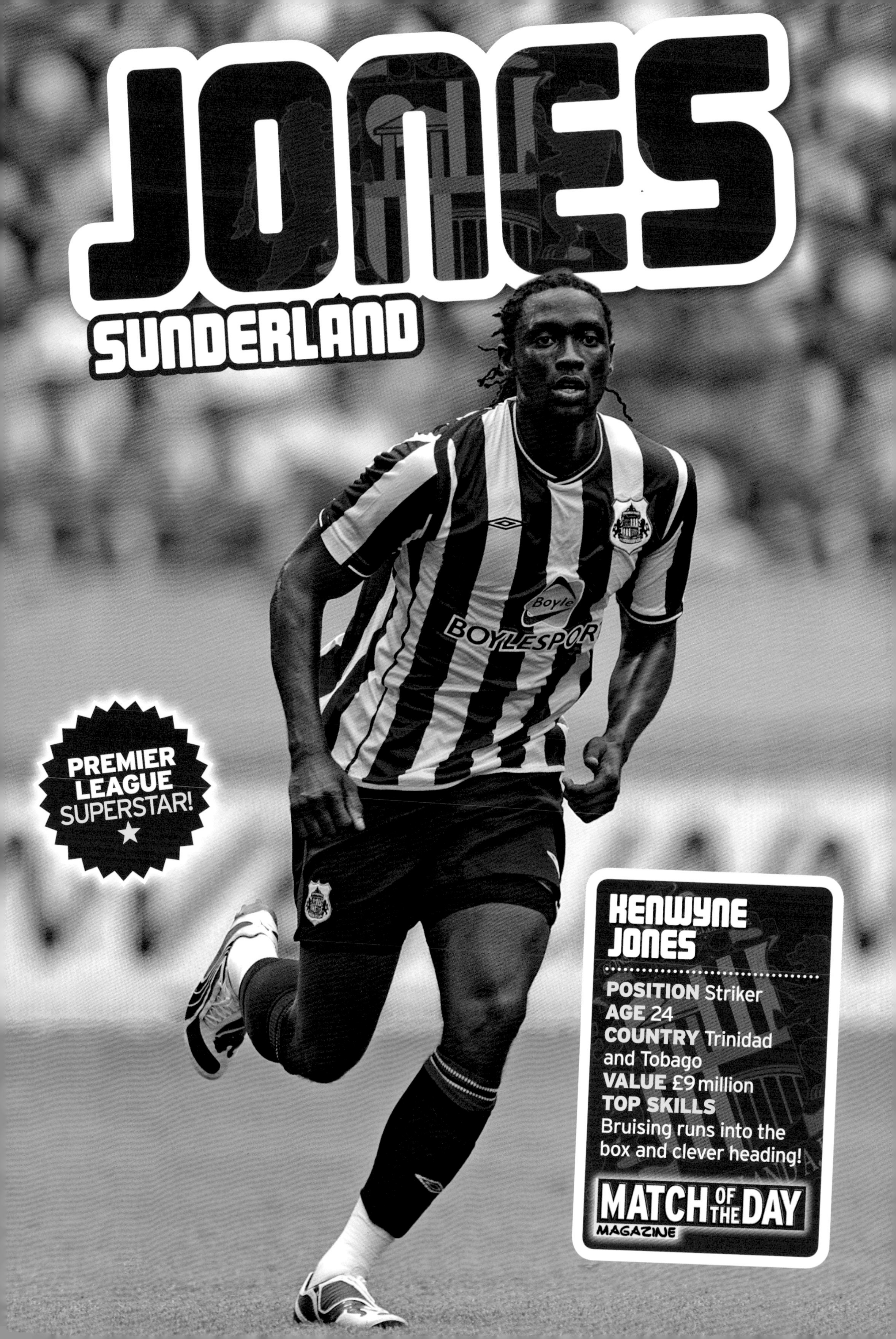

JONES
SUNDERLAND

PREMIER LEAGUE SUPERSTAR!

KENWYNE JONES

POSITION Striker
AGE 24
COUNTRY Trinidad and Tobago
VALUE £9 million
TOP SKILLS Bruising runs into the box and clever heading!

MATCH OF THE DAY
MAGAZINE

10 REASONS WHY WE LOVE... WORLD CUP

MOTD reveals why the 2010 World Cup will be the best ever!

1 FOOTY ON TV!
After school, at the weekend, in fact, every time you turn your telly on during the World Cup there'll be some wicked live footy going on! Make sure you tune in to Match of the Day because Gary Lineker and the boys will be out in South Africa bringing you all the action!

2 NEW STARS!
The World Cup is the best place for exciting young players to show off their skills! In 1998 Michael Owen exploded onto the world scene – could 2010 be the chance for Theo Walcott, Jack Wilshere or Alexandre Pato to shine?

3 HOST NATION!
It's wicked when the host nation does well at the World Cup because their fans start going mental and the atmosphere in the stadiums takes the roof off!

4 FLASH STADIUMS!
Before any country gets to host the World Cup they have to promise FIFA they'll build some mega hi-tech stadiums fit for world superstars! Check out the King Senzangakhona Stadium in Durban, South Africa - it's got a mega arch just like Wembley and holds 70,000 fans!

2010!

5 PENALTY SHOOT-OUTS!
They're rubbish when your side loses, but if you win, it's the best feeling in the world! If any games in the knockout stages are still level after extra-time, they'll go to pens – let's hope England have been practising their spot-kicks!

6 GOLDEN BOOT
World Cup footy means guaranteed goals! You just know Fernando Torres will be scoring crucial goals, but he'll be in competition with his team-mate David Villa and Brazil's deadly front man Luis Fabiano!

7 THE BEST PLAYERS!
It's on the biggest stage where the best players turn on the style – and it doesn't get much bigger than the World Cup! We can't wait to see Kaka, Xavi and Rooney all battling it out to win the biggest prize in footy!

8 EXTRA-TIME DRAMA!
The knockout stages can get so tense you might find yourself hiding behind the sofa to keep calm! In 2006 Italy dumped Germany out of the semis with two awesome late goals in extra-time!

9 CRAZY FANS!
South Africa's nickname – 'Bafana Bafana' – means 'The Boys' and these boys definitely know how to throw a party! The Bafana Bafana fans will be dancing, singing and going crazy non-stop!

10 MOTD MAG!
Don't miss Match of the Day magazine every Tuesday leading up to, and during, the tournament! We'll be bringing you the best World Cup build-up, including the latest action from South Africa and red-hot interviews!

TURN OVER FOR ENGLAND'S WORLD CUP HIGHLIGHTS!

ENGLAND HEROES!

Match of the Day looks back at England's World Cup history!

1966 WORLD CUP WINNERS!
Sir Geoff Hurst is still the only man to score a hat-trick in a World Cup final – his three goals sealed England's 4-2 extra-time win over West Germany!

1990 GAZZA'S TEARS!
England got to the semi-finals at Italia '90! Paul Gascoigne was one of the stars of the summer, but he couldn't stop crying when England lost to Germany on penalties!

1998 MICHAEL OWEN'S GOAL!
Owen was only 17 at France '98, but he skipped past three Argentina defenders and buried a rasping shot in the top corner to score one of the greatest World Cup goals ever!

1998 BECKHAM OFF!
With the scores at 2-2 and England chasing a winner, David Beckham got sent off for kicking an Argentina player!

2002 BECKS' REVENGE!
Four years later England faced Argentina in the group stages. This time it was a different story – Becks thumped an early penalty into the back of Argentina's to seal a massive 1-0 win!

WORLD CUP RECORD!

Check out how far England have done in the last five World Cups!

1990	1994	1998	2002	2006
Semi-final	Didn't qualify	Second round	Quarter-final	Quarter-final

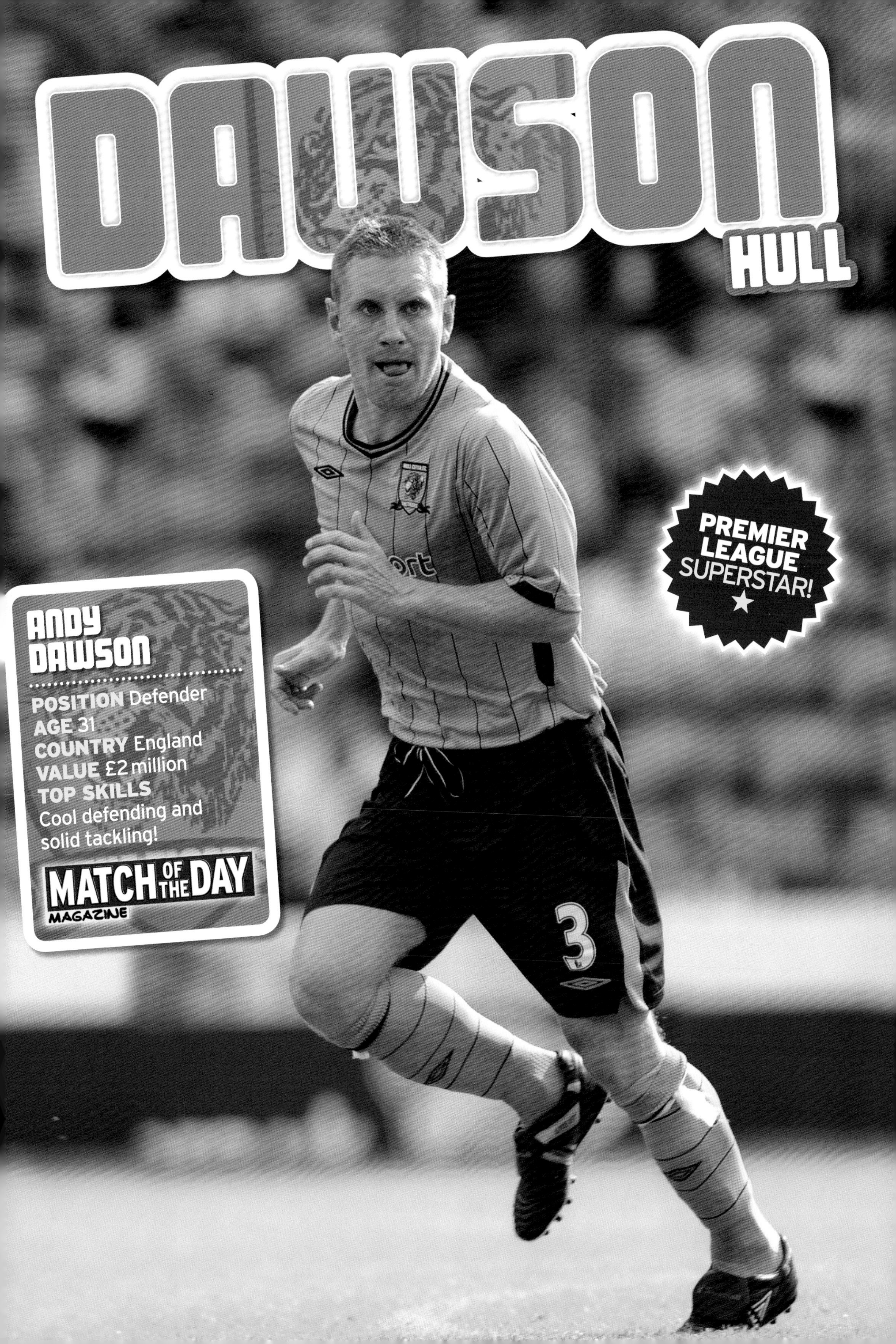

DAWSON
HULL
PREMIER LEAGUE SUPERSTAR!
ANDY DAWSON
POSITION Defender
AGE 31
COUNTRY England
VALUE £2 million
TOP SKILLS
Cool defending and solid tackling!
MATCH OF THE DAY MAGAZINE

LAM

MOTD catches up with Chelsea and En

PARTY AT JT'S!

Do you hang out at other player's houses, Frank?

FRANK SAYS: "Yeah, John Terry's place is really nice - and it's right round the corner from our training ground! He loves throwing barbecues for all the lads in his back garden!"

Have you got loads of footy mates?

FRANK SAYS: "My best mates are the boys I played with at West Ham. You form a special bond with the lads in the academy there. I'm really close to Joe Cole - we're better mates than ever now, and I see Rio Ferdinand and Michael Carrick whenever I'm in Manchester!"

BIG PALS!

PARD!

...and legend Frank Lampard to find out what goes on in his world!

LOVES HIS JOB!

What's the best thing about being a footballer?

FRANK SAYS: "It's quite simple – doing a job you love! You do get some nice things from it – people want to congratulate you and be your mate, but the best thing about it is just coming in to play football every day!"

What's the most-played tune on your iPod?

FRANK SAYS: "When I'm relaxing at home I'll listen to Razorlight or Coldplay, but on the way to a game I like a bit of R'n'B or hip-hop because it really gets you up for the game!"

RAZORLIGHT ROCK!

SPEEDY TEXTER!

So, who's always texting you?

FRANK SAYS: "That'd be either John Terry or Rio Ferdinand. Rio's text-mad. You've got no chance of him answering your calls, but he'll always text back straight away!"

What's the best perk you've had lately?

FRANK SAYS: "I know England cricketer Kevin Pietersen and the other day he got me tickets to go to an England one-day game! He's a top bloke!"

CRICKET MATE!

FRANK'S PHOTO ALBUM!

ON HOLIDAY WITH JT!

GETTING MOBBED BY FANS!

MEETING PRINCESS EUGENIE!

SPLASHING OUT ON NEW GEAR!

DRESSING UP FOR DINNER!

MOTTY'S QUIZ!
WORLD CUP CRAZY!

Count down to the 2010 World Cup with this wicked quiz! Give yourself one point for each correct answer!

1 Which country won the 2006 World Cup in Germany?

YOU SAY ....

2 How many times have England won the tournament?

YOU SAY ....

3 Man. United star Park Ji-Sung plays for which country?

YOU SAY ....

4 True or false? Spain have never won the World Cup!

YOU SAY ....

5 How many teams are in each group at the World Cup finals?

YOU SAY ....

6 How many World Cups has David Beckham played in?

YOU SAY ....

7 True or False? MOTD expert Gary Lineker was top scorer at the 1986 World Cup in Mexico?

YOU SAY ....

8 How many countries has the ex-Chelsea manager Guus Hiddink managed at the World Cup?

YOU SAY ....

9 Which country has won the World Cup more than any other?

YOU SAY ....

10 Which Premier League star is the captain of Germany?

YOU SAY ....

FINAL SCORE...
OUT OF 10

ANSWERS

(DON'T CHEAT!)

MORE QUIZ FUN ON PAGE 76!

SEE HOW MANY YOU GOT RIGHT!
1 Italy, 2 Once, 3 South Korea, 4 True, 5 Four, 6 Three, 7 True, 8 Three, 9 Brazil, 10 Michael Ballack.

66

McFADDEN
BIRMINGHAM

PREMIER LEAGUE SUPERSTAR!

JAMES McFADDEN

POSITION Forward
AGE 26
COUNTRY Scotland
VALUE £5 million
TOP SKILLS
Quality close control
and lethal finishing!

MATCH OF THE DAY
MAGAZINE

FOOTY MAD!

The England stars are enjoying the snow!

Illustration Steve McGarry

LAWRENCE
STOKE

LIAM LAWRENCE

POSITION Midfielder
AGE 27
COUNTRY Republic of Ireland
VALUE £3 million
TOP SKILLS Long-range shooting and ace free-kicks!

MATCH OF THE **DAY**
MAGAZINE

PREMIER LEAGUE SUPERSTAR!
★

Super Skills! PLAY LI CLASS K

Match of the Day reveals how to be a world-class keeper like these awesome players!

1

Amazing Real Madrid and Spain keeper Iker Casillas is awesome at making diving saves...

Keep your arms far out in front of you and get your hands behind the ball! Try to hold on to the ball – but if you can't, push it away from the goal so that a striker doesn't score from the rebound!

2

Edwin van der Sar helps the Man. United defence by coming out to catch crosses...

...focus on the ball and ignore the players around you when you jump! Try to catch the ball at the highest point possible!

KE A... EEPER!

5 TOP KEEPERS

3 Chelsea keeper Petr Cech is well hard to beat from one-on-ones…

…race towards the striker as fast as you can to put him off. Then be brave and dive to the ground to block the ball!

4 Italy and Juventus keeper Gianluigi Buffon knows you have to boss your box to keep a clean sheet…

…shout to your defence if you see an unmarked striker! If the ball comes near you, shout out "Keeper's" so your team-mates give you room to collect it!

For more skills advice, read Match of the Day magazine every week!

SHAY GIVEN
Man. City
Top skill: Catching tricky crosses!

PEPE REINA
Liverpool
Top skill: Savin penalties!

IGOR AKINFEEV
CSKA Moscow
Top skill: Mega-flash dives!

TIM HOWARD
Everton
Top skill: Cleve positioning!

MARK SCHWARZER
Fulham
Top skill: Sharp reflexes!

THE BEST FOOTY NICKNAMES!

MOTD reveals what the top stars are called by their team-mates!

ALEX

Chelsea

What's his nickname? The Tank
Why? Because he's powerful and smashes through anything!

Get outta my way!

THE TANK!

GOOSE!

I'll peck your eyes out!

DAN GOSLING

Everton

What's his nickname? Goose
Why? Because gosling is the name for a baby goose!

THE BEAST!

Don't mess with me!

JULIO BAPTISTA

Roma

What's his nickname? The Beast
Why? Because he's one scary fella!

Let's rain dance!

THE LITTLE CHIEF!

JAVIER MASCHERANO

Liverpool

What's his nickname? The Little Chief
Why? Because he might be small - but he still bosses the midfield!

What's going on with... England?

David Beckham is at Fabio Capello's house...

You got any jobs for me to do, gaffer?

Well, you can paint my porch!

Okay! Leave it to me!

One hour later...

Nooooo! What have you done, Becks?

I told you to paint my Porch!

Oops! I thought you said Porsche!

Illustration Paul Cemmick

EBANKS-BLAKE
WOLVES

PREMIER LEAGUE SUPERSTAR!
★

SYLVAN EBANKS-BLAKE

POSITION Striker
AGE 23
COUNTRY England
VALUE £6 million
TOP SKILLS
Massive strength and powerful shooting!

MATCH OF THE **DAY**
MAGAZINE

HOW TO BE A...
FOOTY SUP

Match of the Day checks out the most stylish stars in footy!

The coolest footy stars in Manchester wear red!

Does this jacket look all-white?

Er, don't you mean blue, Wazza?

FLASH ROBBIE TWO-COLLARS!

LITTLE RED ROONEY HOOD!

BELT UP, MATE!

CHECK OUT RON'S TWO PHONES!

ROBINHO
Man. City

WAYNE ROONEY
Man. United

CRISTIANO RONALDO
Real Madrid

...ERSTAR!

I look like James Bond!

DAVID BECKHAM
LA Galaxy

LICENCE TO SKILL?

I could play for Brazil in this!

OLYMPIC GOLD MEDAL?

NIC'S PRETTY SLICK!

NICOLAS ANELKA
Chelsea

My jeans are well old!

EL-HADJI DIOUF
Blackburn

Check out my hat-trick, dudes!

MICAH RICHARDS
Man. City

Like my pink bag, lads?

PETER CROUCH
Tottenham

SPOT THE DIFFERENCE!

Circle the five differences between each pair of pictures and bag a point for each difference you can find!

FINAL SCORE...
OUT OF 10

MORE QUIZ FUN ON PAGE 84!

DAVIES
BOLTON

PREMIER LEAGUE SUPERSTAR!
★

KEVIN DAVIES

POSITION Forward
AGE 32
COUNTRY England
VALUE £4 million
TOP SKILLS
Mega strength and bullet headers!

MATCH OF THE **DAY**
MAGAZINE

MATCH OF THE DAY
EXPERT QU

How much do you know about Match of the Day's wicked footy experts?

GOAL KING GARY!

1 Gary Lineker played 80 games for England – have a guess at how many goals he scored for his country!

A 8   B 18   C 28   D 48

2 Which of these Prem clubs did Lineker play for?

A Tottenham   B Man. United

C Aston Villa   D West Ham

BARCA BOY!

3 True or false? Barcelona was the only Spanish team that Gary played for!

A True

B False

GARY STRIKES AGAIN!

4 Which club is Lineker playing for in this pic?

A Chelsea

B Man. City

C Everton

D Birmingham

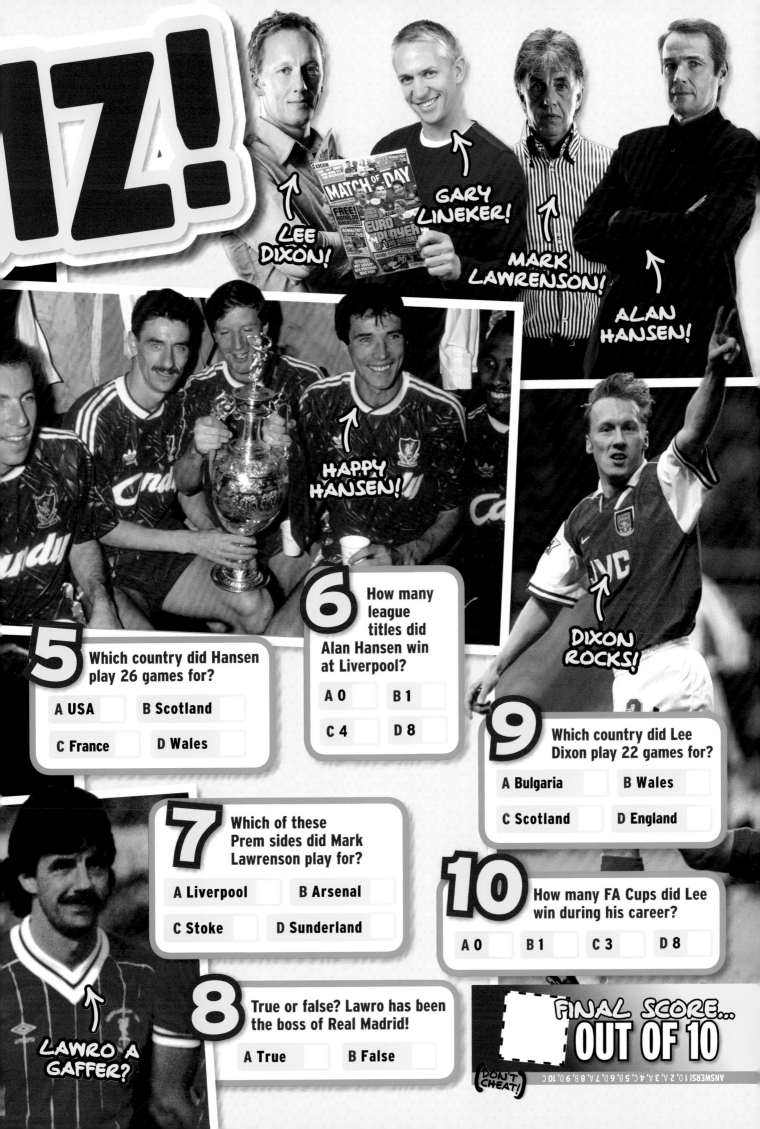

1Z4!

LEE DIXON!

GARY LINEKER!

MARK LAWRENSON!

ALAN HANSEN!

HAPPY HANSEN!

DIXON ROCKS!

LAWRO A GAFFER?

5 Which country did Hansen play 26 games for?

A USA
B Scotland
C France
D Wales

6 How many league titles did Alan Hansen win at Liverpool?

A 0
B 1
C 4
D 8

7 Which of these Prem sides did Mark Lawrenson play for?

A Liverpool
B Arsenal
C Stoke
D Sunderland

8 True or false? Lawro has been the boss of Real Madrid!

A True
B False

9 Which country did Lee Dixon play 22 games for?

A Bulgaria
B Wales
C Scotland
D England

10 How many FA Cups did Lee win during his career?

A 0
B 1
C 3
D 8

FINAL SCORE...
OUT OF 10

(DON'T CHEAT!)

ANSWERS! 1 D, 2 A, 3 A, 4 C, 5 B, 6 D, 7 A, 8 B, 9 D, 10 C

PREM SUPERKIDS OF 2010!

Match of the Day reveals the five youngsters who can become superstars over the next 12 months!

JACK WILSHERE

CLUB: Arsenal **POSITION:** Midfielder

AGE: 17 **COUNTRY:** England

HE'S THE NEW: Kaka!

MOTD SAYS: Jack's the real deal – make no mistake! We just love watching his silky dribbling skills, defence-splitting passes and long-range curlers!

GUNNER BE AWESOME!

WARNING! PREM SUPERSTAR ALERT!

HOT ROD!

JACK RODWELL

CLUB: Everton **POSITION:** Midfielder/Centre-back

AGE: 18 **COUNTRY:** England **HE'S THE NEW:** Rio Ferdinand!

MOTD SAYS: This boy is pure class – you'd never guess he is so young! He's cool and composed under pressure, a wicked passer of the ball and always reads the game brilliantly!

DANNY WELBECK

CLUB: Man.United

POSITION: Striker

AGE: 18 **COUNTRY:** England

HE'S THE NEW: Emmanuel Adebayor!

MOTD SAYS: Danny's got everything – but it's his pace and power that catches the eye! Don't be surprised if he makes England's World Cup squad!

WICKED PROSPECT!

LETHAL STRIKER!

KRISZTIAN NEMETH

CLUB: Liverpool **POSITION:** Striker **AGE:** 20

COUNTRY: Hungary **HE'S THE NEW:** David Villa!

MOTD SAYS: A surprise choice perhaps – but he's lethal in front of goal! Give him one chance and he'll gobble it up. He could become an Anfield legend!

DANIEL STURRIDGE

CLUB: Chelsea **POSITION:** Striker **AGE:** 20

COUNTRY: England **HE'S THE NEW:** Samuel Eto'o!

MOTD SAYS: We spotted Daniel a couple of years ago – and we reckon he's going to blow up in 2010! He's razor-sharp and has some of the sickest skills around!

NEW BLUES FAVE!

JAMES
PORTSMOUTH

PREMIER LEAGUE SUPERSTAR! ★

DAVID JAMES
....
POSITION Keeper
AGE 39
COUNTRY England
VALUE £1million
TOP SKILLS
Mega shot stopping and blocking one-on-ones!

MATCH OF THE **DAY**
MAGAZINE

WHICH PLAYER

Find out which footy superstar YOU are with this awesome quiz!

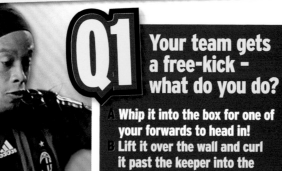

DEAD-BALL WIZARD?

FLAIR FOR HAIR?

Q1 Your team gets a free-kick - what do you do?

A Whip it into the box for one of your forwards to head in!
B Lift it over the wall and curl it past the keeper into the top corner!
C Look for your tallest striker and launch a long one onto his head!
D Fire it high over the bar and get in a huff with your team-mates for putting you off!
E By the time you've waddled over the free-kick has been taken and you're too late!

Q2 How often do you change your haircut?

A You switch between a mullet and the classic short look!
B Four times a year - you've got to stay ahead of everybody else!
C Your mum tells the barber what to do!
D Never! A hairband does the job!
E Every time you find a bit of food stuck in there!

Q3 You've just won the World Cup - what do you do now?

A Quietly celebrate with your best mates!
B Get your whole family on the pitch and smile for the cameras!
C Go home and read Harry Potter!
D Grab the cup and put it in your trophy cabinet!
E Slouch on the sofa and watch a bit of TV!

Q4 What do you want for Christmas?

A A new footy so you can practise your passing!
B A flash limited edition Bugatti Veyron!
C The best keeper gloves available on the market!
D A mirror to look at yourself!
E A massive box of chocolates!

ARE YOU?

Q6

GOAL CRAZY?

How do you celebrate scoring a goal?

A With a massive scream!
B Run with your arms out!
C Me, score a goal? You must be joking!
D Point to yourself and shout "I'm the man!"
E Stroll to the half-way line for kick-off!

Q5

Do you like pies?

A No way - it's all about nice Spanish paella for me!
B If they're served with a dollop of mash!
C I prefer a nice plate of Irish Stew!
D Yuk! Bring me a croissant!
E I love pies, me!

Q7

DREAM GIRL?

Describe your dream WAG...

A A Spanish senorita with long, dark hair!
B A famous pop star who's always in the gossip columns!
C Pale skin, blue eyes and no celeb pals!
D Someone who knows I'm always right!
E Anyone who'll have me!

Q8

Who would be your perfect team-mate?

A Someone who's a slick passer!
B A tall striker who heads in your crosses!
C A defender who's ace at last-ditch tackles!
D Who needs team-mates? I've got the skills to take on anyone!
E A full-back who'll do my defending for me!

PERFECT PAL?

WHAT DID YOU TICK THE MOST?

MOSTLY As...
CESC FABREGAS!
You're a classy midfielder who plays footy the right way - with loads of stylish passing!

MOSTLY Bs...
DAVID BECKHAM!
You love grabbing the headlines - you're a fashionable star and a set-piece king!

MOSTLY Cs...
SHAY GIVEN!
You're a safe pair of hands in goal and you never cause the team any problems!

MOSTLY Ds...
DIDIER DROGBA!
Talk about a prima donna! You're so confident, you think you're the only player on the pitch!

MOSTLY Es...
ANDY REID!
It's time to shape up, get on the treadmill and get fit for footy!

HOT WHEELS?

SPOT THE BALL!

There are loads of balls in these pictures! Guess which one is the real one in each and get 25 points for a right answer!

ANSWERS

(DON'T CHEAT!)

SEE HOW MANY YOU GOT RIGHT!
Arsenal v Fulham – 2E,
Chelsea v Blackburn – 4E,
Liverpool v Hull – 5E,
Aston Villa v QPR – 2E

FINAL SCORE...
OUT OF 100

MORE QUIZ FUN ON PAGE 88!

RODALLEGA
WIGAN

PREMIER LEAGUE SUPERSTAR!

HUGO RODALLEGA

POSITION Striker
AGE 24
COUNTRY Colombia
VALUE £6 million
TOP SKILLS
Powerful running and explosive shooting!

MEGA MA[TCH]

DERBY BATTLE!

6 FEBRUARY

LIVERPOOL V EVERTON

COMPETITION: PREMIER LEAGUE

The Merseyside neighbours are always hard to separate – the last two meetings at Anfield ended 1-1!

CARLING CUP FINAL

COMPETITION: CARLING CUP

It's the first chance for silverware of the season and it's the 50th League Cup final! A place in Europe is also up for grabs for the winners!

28 FEBRUARY

MAN. UNITED V LIVERPOOL

COMPETITION: PREMIER LEAGUE

This is a massive game in the title race! United will also want to get revenge after losing 4-1 at home to Liverpool last season!

20 MARCH

TOTTENHAM V ARSENAL

COMPETITION: PREMIER LEAGUE

North London will be totally divided when Tottenham try to beat Arsenal in the Prem for the first time since November 1999!

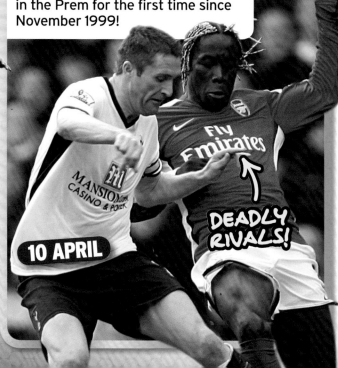

DEADLY RIVALS!

10 APRIL

MAN. UNITED V CHELSEA

3 APRIL

COMPETITION: PREMIER LEAGUE

With only a month of the season to go, this mega clash could decide who will get their hands on the Premier League title!

TCHES! 2010

MEGA SCRAP!

17 APRIL

MAN. CITY V MAN. UNITED

COMPETITION: PREMIER LEAGUE

This won't be just a Manchester derby – it'll be an awesome display of attacking football from these two sharp-shooting giants!

ASTON VILLA V BIRMINGHAM

24 APRIL

COMPETITION: PREMIER LEAGUE

Birmingham return to local rivals Aston Villa for the first time since April 2008 and will hope to climb up the table!

FA CUP FINAL

COMPETITION: FA CUP

Expect loads of twists and turns leading to the FA Cup final! Chelsea won't want to give up the trophy without a fight!

15 MAY

Fixtures subject to change

KINGS OF EUROPE!

22 MAY

CHAMPIONS LEAGUE FINAL

COMPETITION: CHAMPIONS LEAGUE

Barcelona picked up the big trophy last May when they beat Man. United! Who will go all the way this time and win the final in Madrid?

THE BIG ONE!

WORLD CUP FINAL

COMPETITION: WORLD CUP

The World Cup kicks off in South Africa on 11 June – and the whole world will be watching the final in Johannesburg on 11 July!

11 JULY

MOTTY'S QUIZ!
LA LIGA STARS!

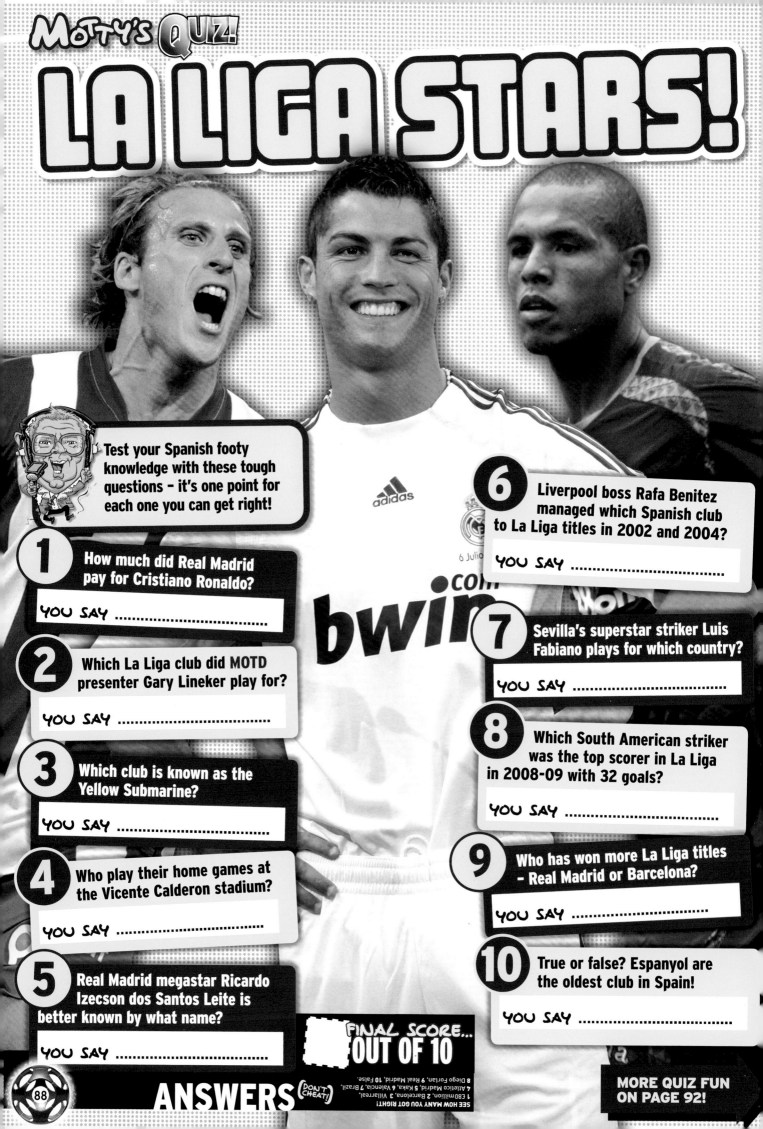

Test your Spanish footy knowledge with these tough questions – it's one point for each one you can get right!

1 How much did Real Madrid pay for Cristiano Ronaldo?

YOU SAY ....

2 Which La Liga club did MOTD presenter Gary Lineker play for?

YOU SAY ....

3 Which club is known as the Yellow Submarine?

YOU SAY ....

4 Who play their home games at the Vicente Calderon stadium?

YOU SAY ....

5 Real Madrid megastar Ricardo Izecson dos Santos Leite is better known by what name?

YOU SAY ....

6 Liverpool boss Rafa Benitez managed which Spanish club to La Liga titles in 2002 and 2004?

YOU SAY ....

7 Sevilla's superstar striker Luis Fabiano plays for which country?

YOU SAY ....

8 Which South American striker was the top scorer in La Liga in 2008-09 with 32 goals?

YOU SAY ....

9 Who has won more La Liga titles – Real Madrid or Barcelona?

YOU SAY ....

10 True or false? Espanyol are the oldest club in Spain!

YOU SAY ....

FINAL SCORE...
OUT OF 10

MORE QUIZ FUN ON PAGE 92!

88

EAGLES

BURNLEY

PREMIER LEAGUE SUPERSTAR! ★

cooke
established 1845

CHRIS EAGLES

POSITION Winger
AGE 23
COUNTRY England
VALUE £3 million
TOP SKILLS
Thumping volleys and speedy dribblng!

MATCH OF **THE DAY**
MAGAZINE

FUN FOOTY GAME...
GOAL CRAZY!

Try to beat your mate by taking your chances and scoring the most goals! Take turns rolling a dice - the number it lands on decides what happens! See who can bag the most goals!

1 You receive the ball in the area, then turn and shoot...

GOAL! The keeper didn't even move!

POST! It falls back at your feet - roll again!

WIDE! That was closer to the club shop than the goal!

GOAL! Excellent finish with the inside of your foot!

SAVED! The keeper palms it back to you - roll again!

OVER! Hey - that hit my gran in the crowd!

PENALTY BOX STRIKE!

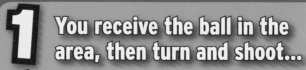

ARE YOU A DEADLY FINISHER?

2 You've been given a penalty! You step up...

GOAL! You smashed it into the top corner!

SAVE! It comes back off the keeper - roll again!

GOAL! Cheeky! You chip it straight down the middle!

OVER! Oh no - that's gone into row Z!

SAVE! The keeper guesses the right way!

GOAL! Your penalty hits the post and goes in!

3 You have a crack from 25 yards out...

SAVED! An awesome stop from the keeper!

BLOCKED! It hits a defender and comes back - roll again!

OVER! Steady - the ball almost hit a plane!

GOAL! What a screamer - in off the post!

POST! You collect the rebound - roll again!

GOAL! The ball deflects off a defender's bum and goes in!

PENALTY PRESSURE!

4 You're through on goal and one-on-one with the keeper...

GOAL! You chipped it over the keeper!

SAVED! It comes back to you – roll again!

GOAL! You dribble past the keeper and stroke it in!

WIDE! Shocking miss! My mum could've scored!

POST! The ball bounces back to you – roll again!

SAVED! Wicked block by the keeper!

HEADING AT GOAL!

ONE-ON-ONE WITH THE KEEPER!

5 You head a cross towards goal...

GOAL! That almost ripped the net!

SAVED! It comes back to you – roll again!

GOAL! You jump really high and head it in!

OVER! That was so close to being a goal!

GOAL! A glancing header into the corner!

WIDE! That nearly hit the corner flag!

6 You step up to hit a free-kick from outside the box...

GOAL! Beautifully curled around the defensive wall!

BLOCKED! It hits the wall and comes back to you – roll again!

SAVED! The keeper makes an awesome diving save!

GOAL! Your rocket free-kick flew past the keeper!

BLOCKED! The wall does its job – roll again!

WIDE! Your clever free-kick whistles just past the post!

FREE-KICK KING!

Full-time! How many goals did you score?

 /6

MOTTY'S QUIZ!
SERIE A QUIZ!

Test your Italian footy knowledge with these ace questions - it's a point for each one you get right!

1 AC and Inter Milan play their home games at which stadium?

YOU SAY ....

2 True or False? West Ham manager Gianfranco Zola once played for Italian club Lazio!

YOU SAY ....

3 AC Milan midfielder Gennaro Gattuso played for which Scottish club when he was younger?

YOU SAY ....

4 Tough-tackling Inter Milan captain Javier Zanetti plays for which international team?

YOU SAY ....

5 Which Serie A club is nicknamed The Old Lady?

YOU SAY ....

6 How many teams are there in Serie A - 18, 20 or 22?

YOU SAY ....

7 Which club has won the Italian league for the past four seasons?

YOU SAY ....

8 Which Serie A playmaker is the captain of Roma?

YOU SAY ....

9 Which Premier League club did Fiorentina striker Adrian Mutu play for between 2003 and 2005?

YOU SAY ....

10 Juventus have won the Serie A title the most! But have they won it 15, 27 or 40 times?

YOU SAY ....

FINAL SCORE...
OUT OF 10

7 THINGS 201[...]

Have a footy-mad 2010, readers!

Tick off these things if you spot them on the pitch!

GETTING SHIRTY!

1 Bellamy getting in a big strop!

Man. City striker Craig Bellamy loves to have a moan on the pitch!

I'VE SEEN IT!

2 Fergie pointing to his watch!

The Man. United boss is always shouting at the ref about how long is left!

I'VE SEEN IT!

3 The ball sticking in Fellaini's hair!

The Everton hero's hair is so big, the ball could easily get lost in it when he goes to head for goal!

I'VE SEEN IT!